so take me someplace far away

四つ葉のクローバー
FOUR-LEAF CLOVER
三つ葉のクローバー
THREE-LEAF CLOVER
歌う声
A SINGER'S VOICE
聞こえる声
AN AUDIBLE VOICE
呼ぶ音
A BECKONING SOUND
通信
COMMUNICATION
約束
A PROMISE
血
BLOOD
一人
ALONE
追われる者
THE HUNTED
追う者
THE HUNTER
線
THE LINE
反応
RESPONSE
蜘蛛の巣
A SPIDER'S WEB
見守る小鳥の歌
A SONG FROM A BIRD TO WATCH OVER ME
帰る場所
A PLACE TO RETURN TO
雨
RAIN
5
FIVE
4
FOUR
3
THREE
信頼
TRUST
任務
DUTY
印
A SIGN
願い
A WISH
クローバーのしあわせ
A CLOVER'S BLISS
髪と睦言
SOFT HAIR AND SWEET NOTHINGS
鏡と接触
A MIRROR AND A TOUCH
苛立ち
IRRITATION
分からないから分かりたい
I WANT TO SEE WHAT I DON'T UNDERSTAND
みんなにうたう歌
A SONG FOR EVERYONE
ふたりできく歌
A SONG FOR TWO
ひとりでうたう歌
A SONG FOR ONE
怒り
ANGER
窓の外
OUTSIDE THE WINDOW
気をつけて
BE CAREFUL
別れ
FAREWELL
涙
TEARS
二葉
TWO-LEAF
生まれ変わる
REBIRTH
C→R
C-R
私も
ME TOO

If you find a fou
You wil
discover happiness

But it can
Never be found

Happiness lies inside
A secret cage

No one can possess
The four-leaf clover

But then,
What of the three-leaf clover?

FOUR-LEAF CLOVER
『四つ葉のクローバー』

The three-leaf Clover...
...is leaving its cage.

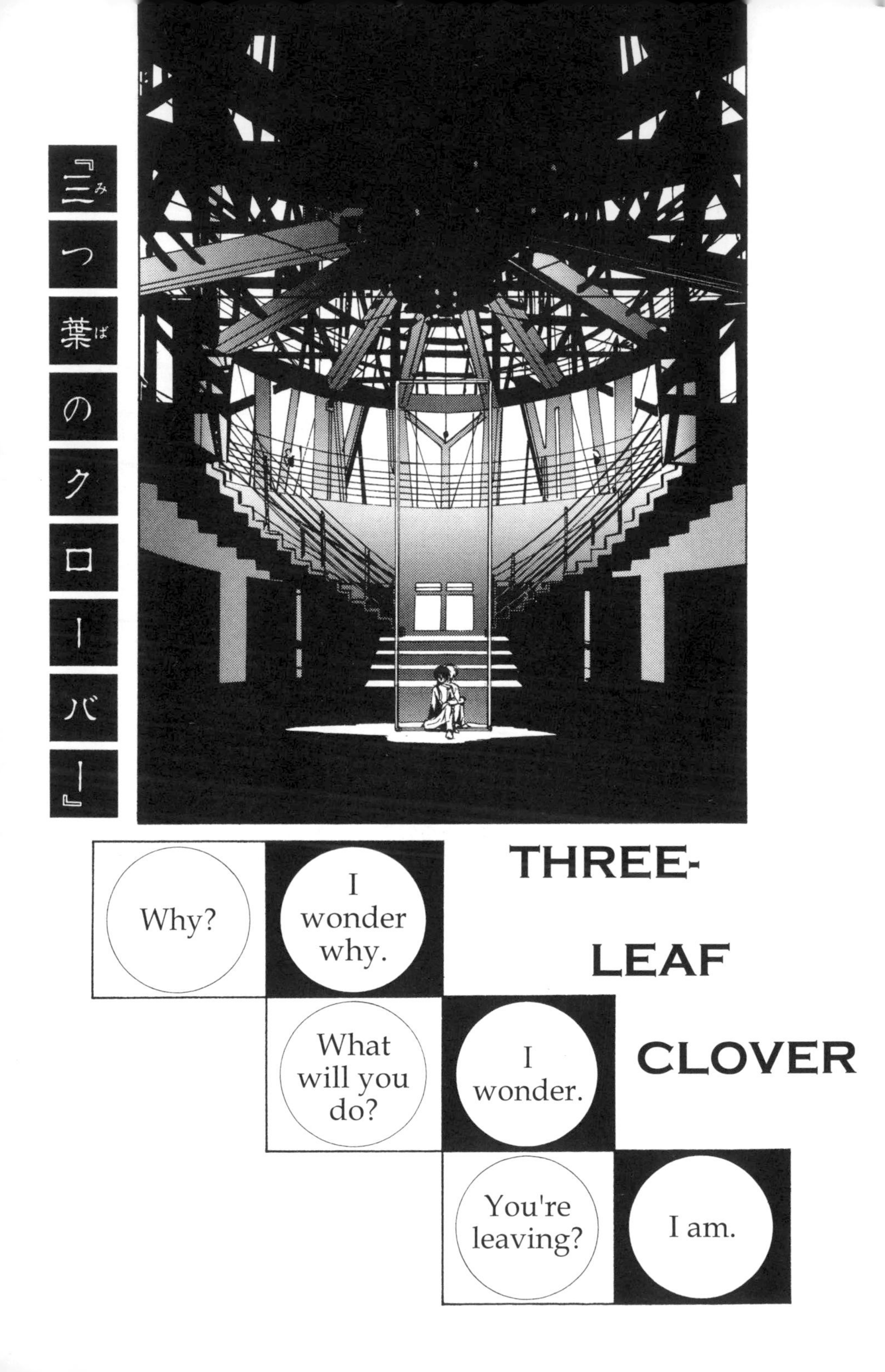
『三つ葉のクローバー』
THREE-LEAF CLOVER
Why?
I wonder why.
What will you do?
I wonder.
You're leaving?
I am.

No matter how much I beg you to stay?
Goodbye.

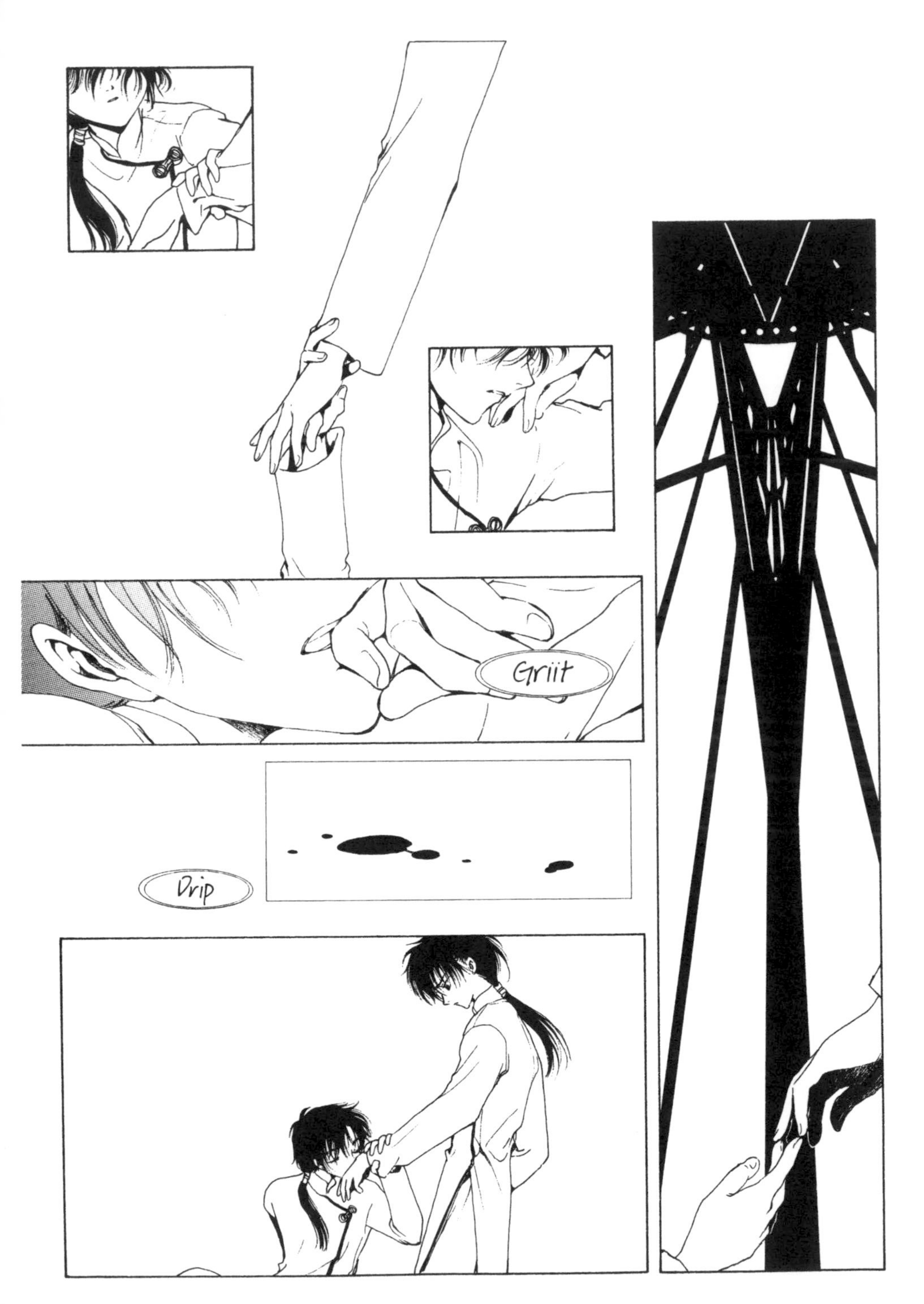
Griit
Drip

I'll see you soon.

For
you I
will be
reborn

『歌う声』 A Singer's Voice

Fearlessly, Unceasingly, Patiently

It took me three months to get her.

In your
arms
I will be
reborn

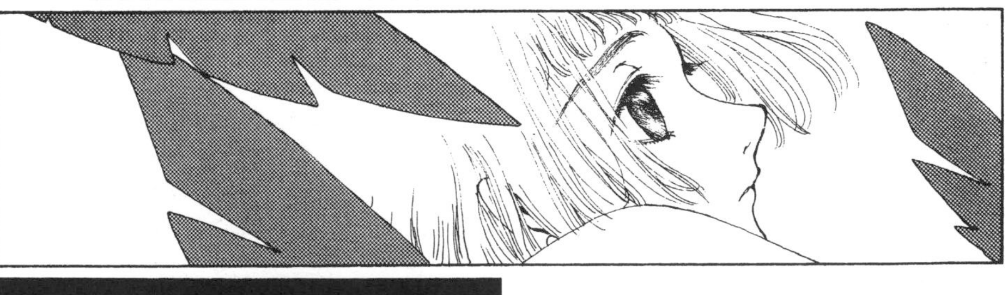

I will be reborn

There were three three-leaf Clovers.
One died.
One remains in the cage.
And the other...
...has departed.
For myself I will be reborn
In your arms I will be reborn

A Beckoning Sound
『呼ぶ音』
This is my commander, Gingetsu.
Hello, I'm Ora.
May I give him a kiss?
And for you...
BEEEEEEEP
Beep
Duty calls?
Yes.
I had hoped we'd get to relax for a while.
Beep

You army guys are always getting called to action.
Yeah, it bothers me.
It means less time I can spend with you.

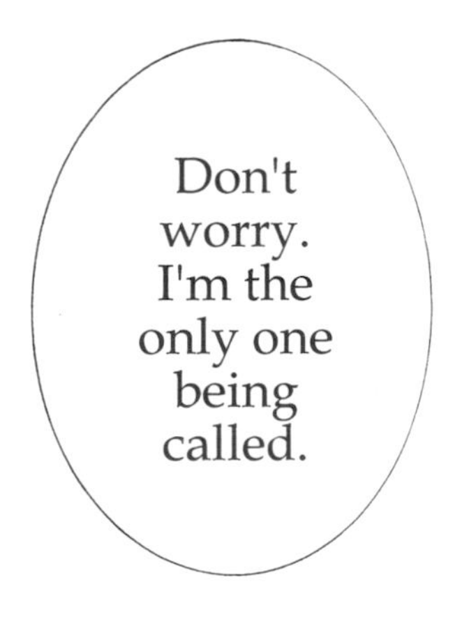
Don't worry. I'm the only one being called.

COMMUNICATION
『通信』
The three-leaf has escaped.
One of them has left the cage.
At least they both didn't escape.
Azaiea hasn't found out yet.
But the real problem is the Council.

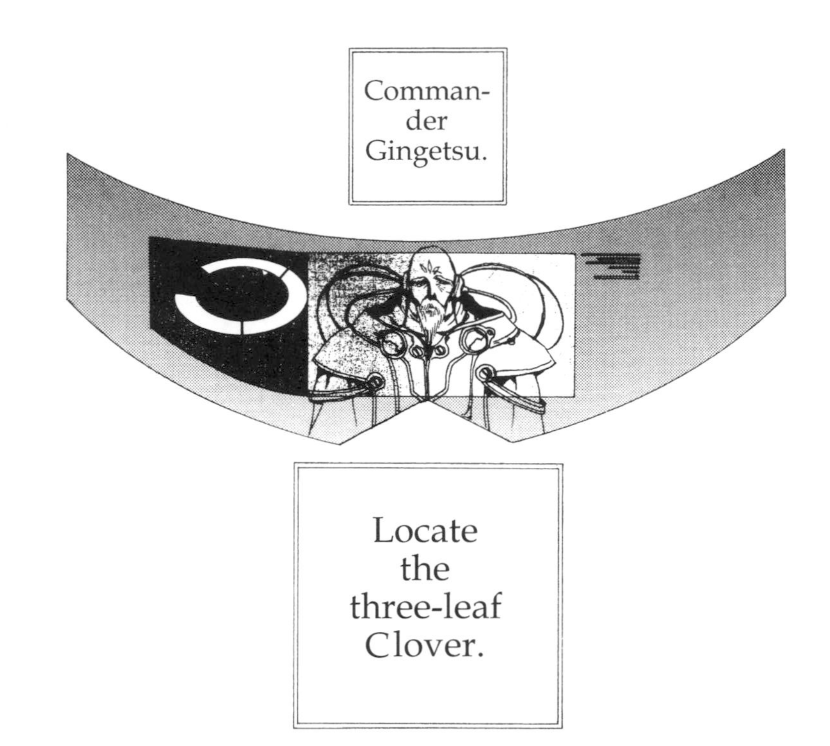
Comman-
der
Gingetsu.
Locate
the
three-leaf
Clover.

A Promise
『約束』
やく
そく
Are you sure...
...you don't have to go?
He and I have a promise.
What kind of promise?
That he won't die before I do.
To not die is the greatest gift you can give someone you love.
What is it?

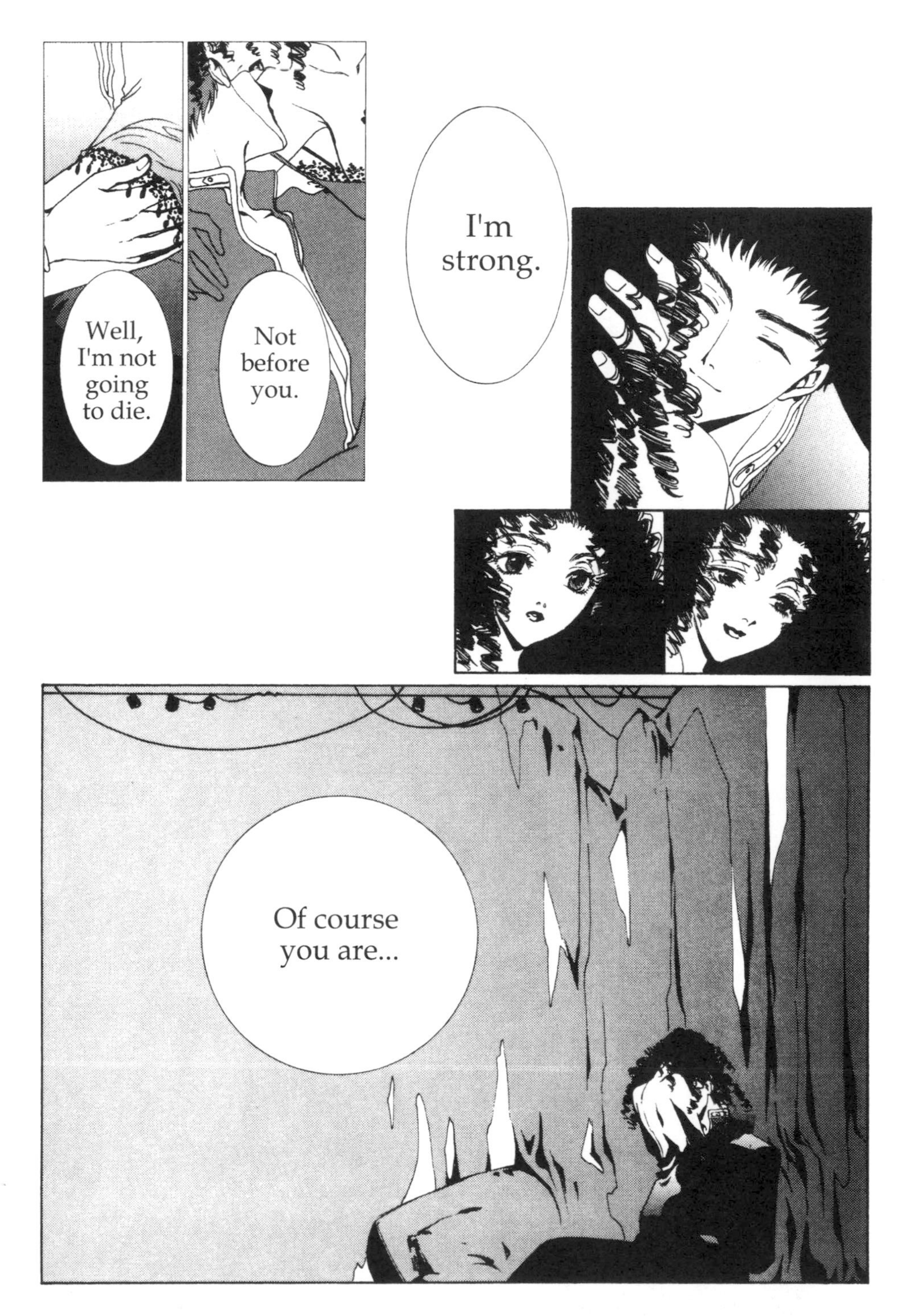
Not before you.
Well, I'm not going to die.
I'm strong.
Of course you are...

BLOOD

And we're the only three-leafs.

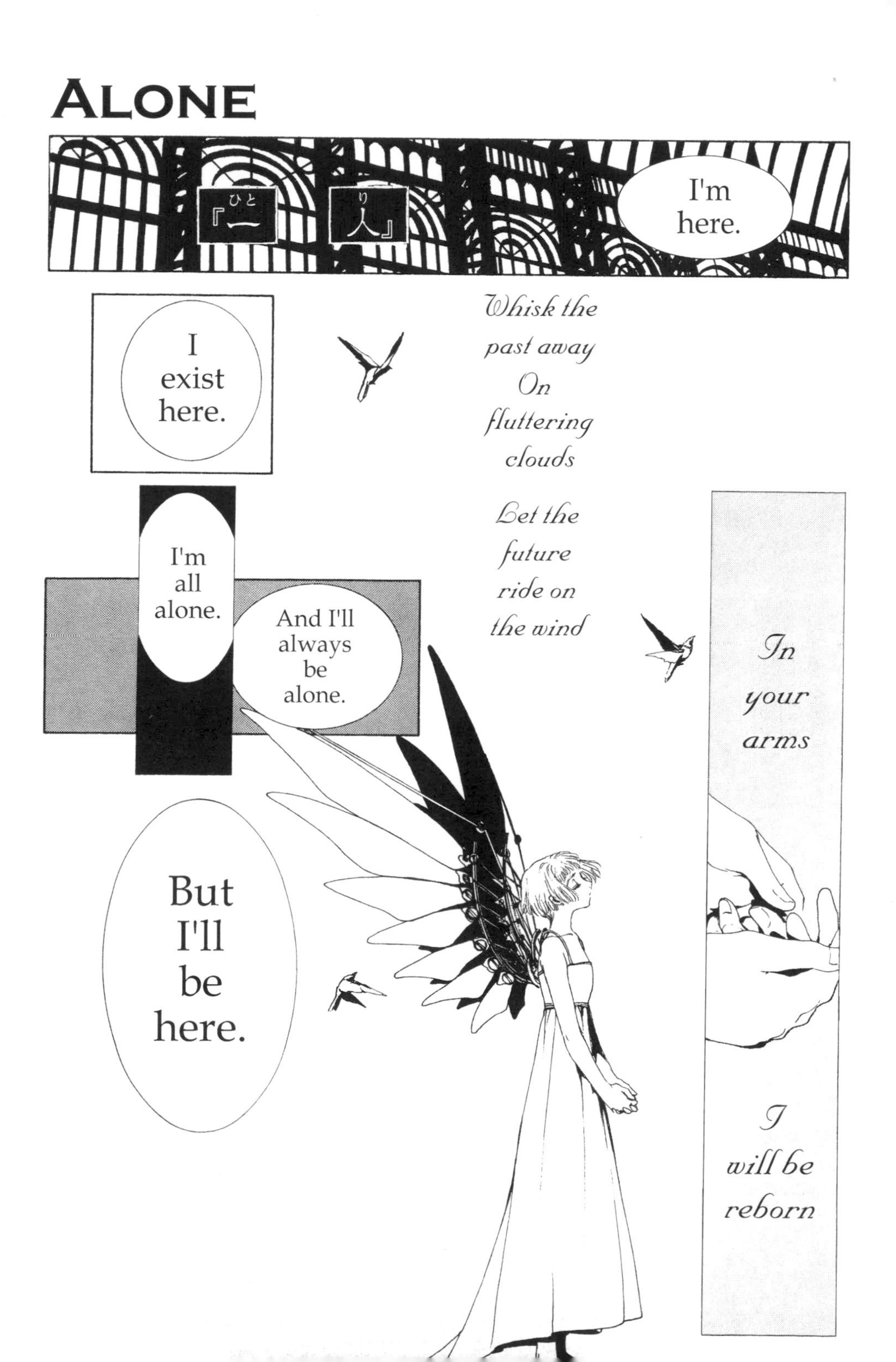
ALONE
『一人』
I'm here.
I exist here.
I'm all alone.
And I'll always be alone.
But I'll be here.
Whisk the past away On fluttering clouds
Let the future ride on the wind
In your arms
I will be reborn

THE HUNTED

『追われる者』

THE HUNTER

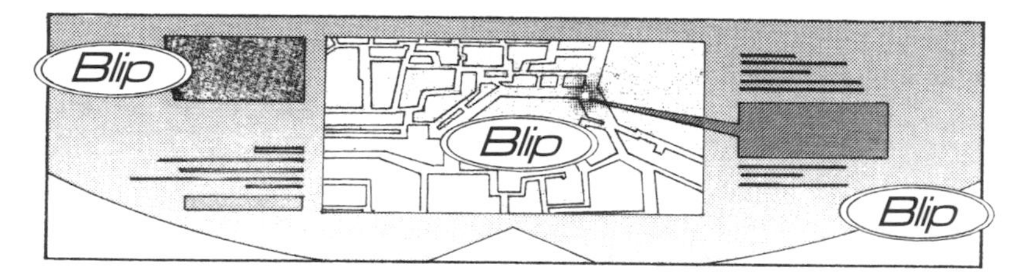

THE LINE
せん
『線』
You must be C.
Come with us.
I'm not going back.

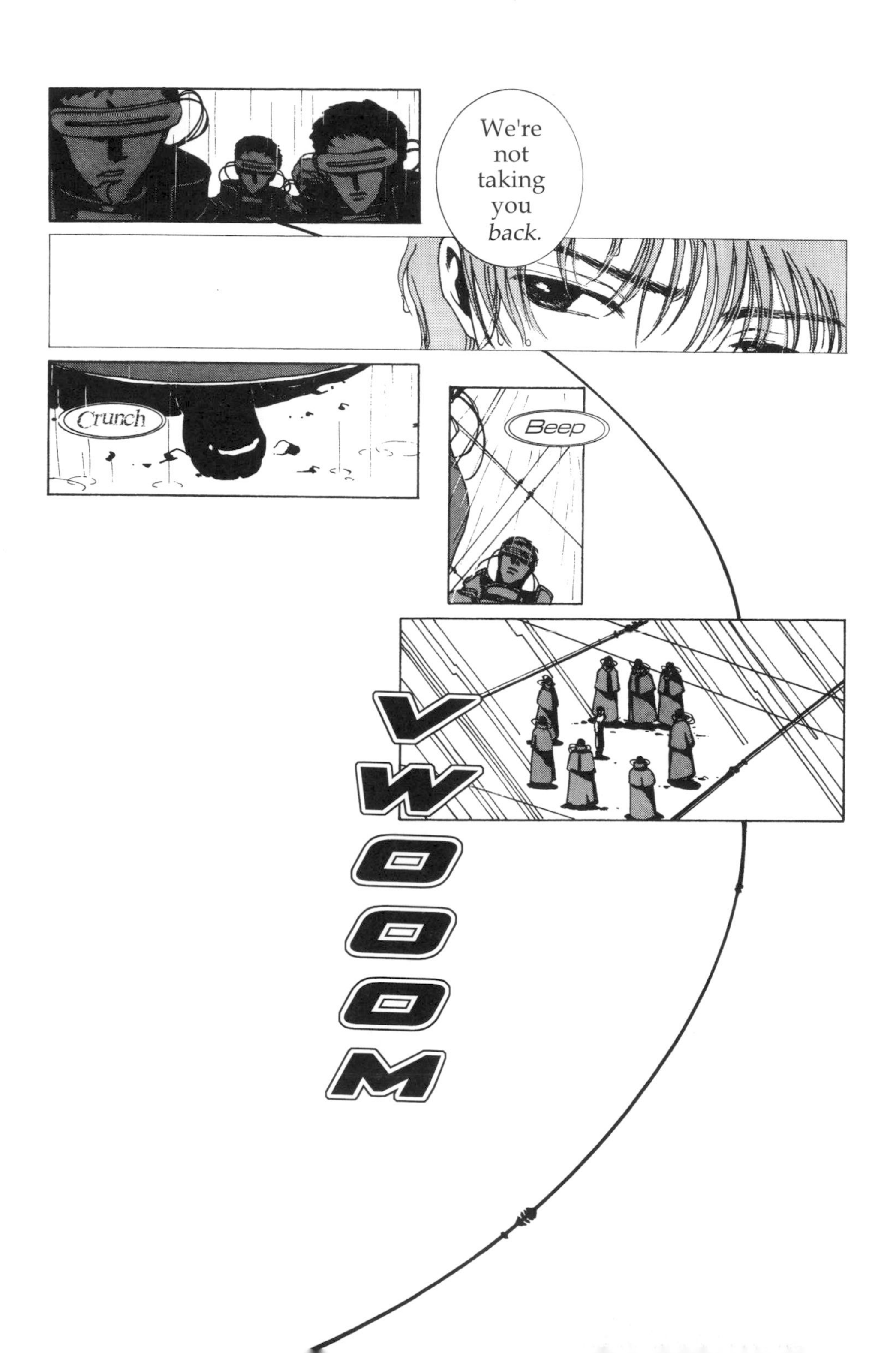

We're not taking you *back*.
Crunch
Beep
VWOOOM

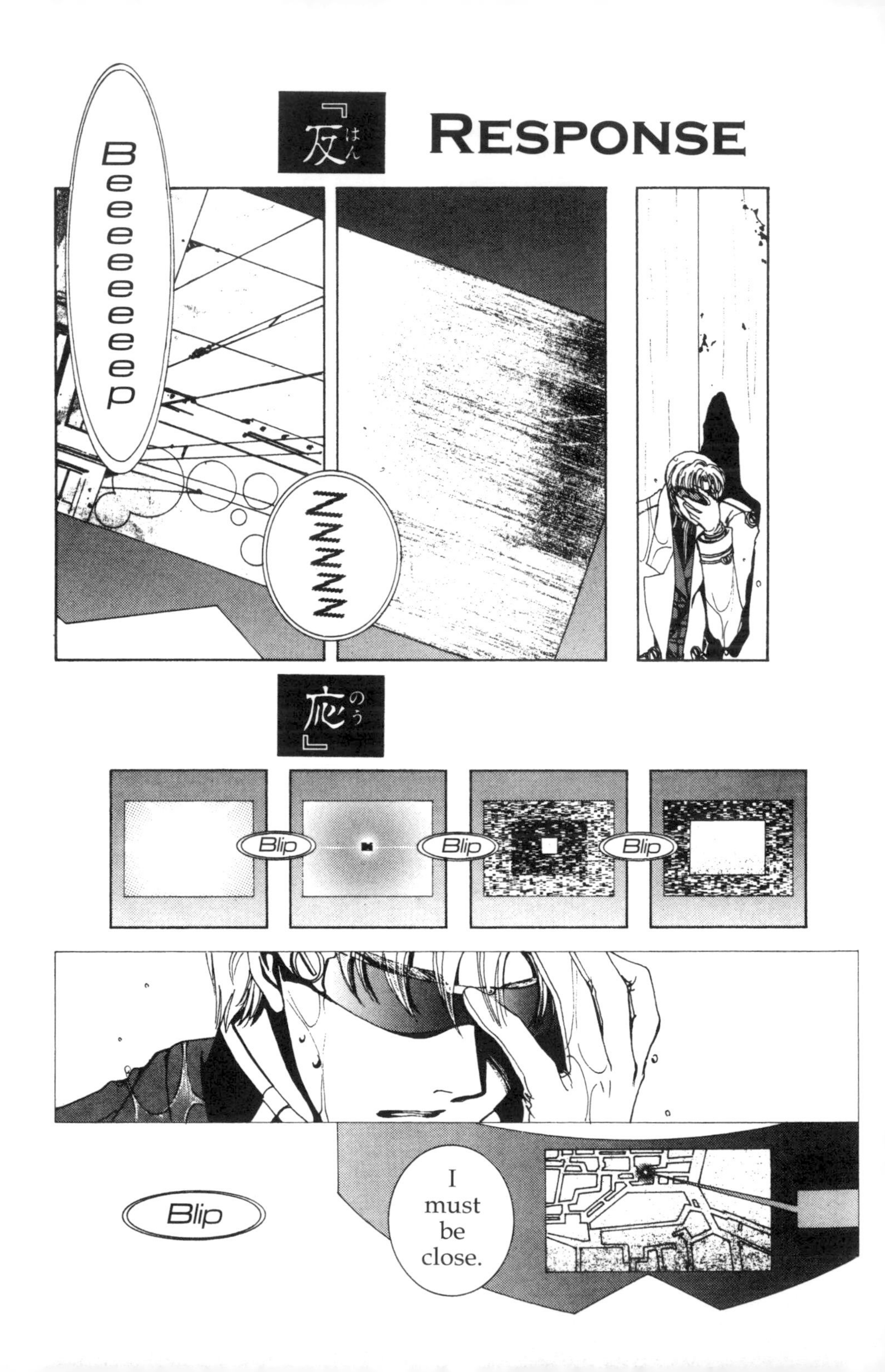
『反応』
RESPONSE
Beeeeeeeeeep
ZZZZZ
Blip
Blip
Blip
Blip
I must be close.

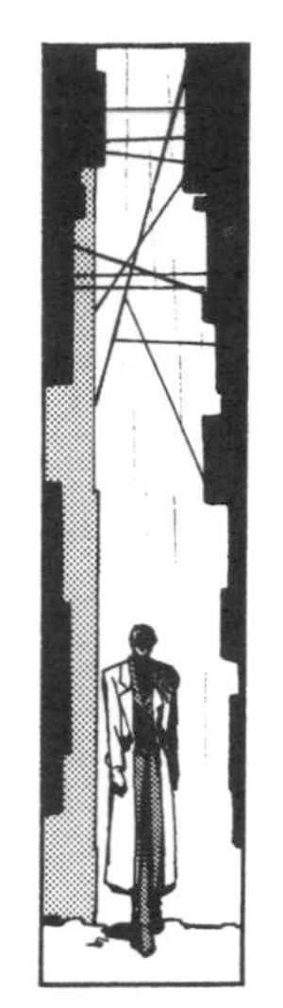

Spider's

Web

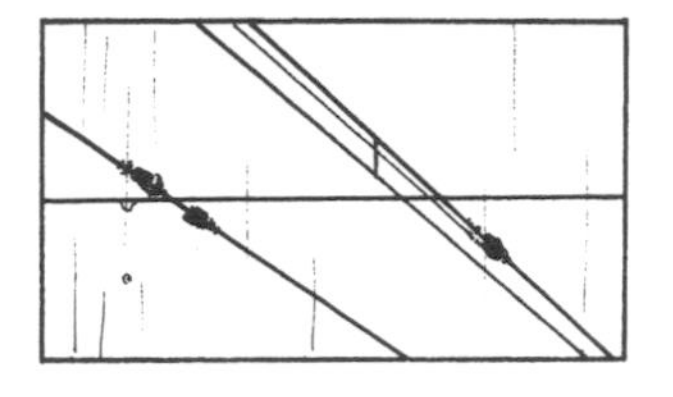

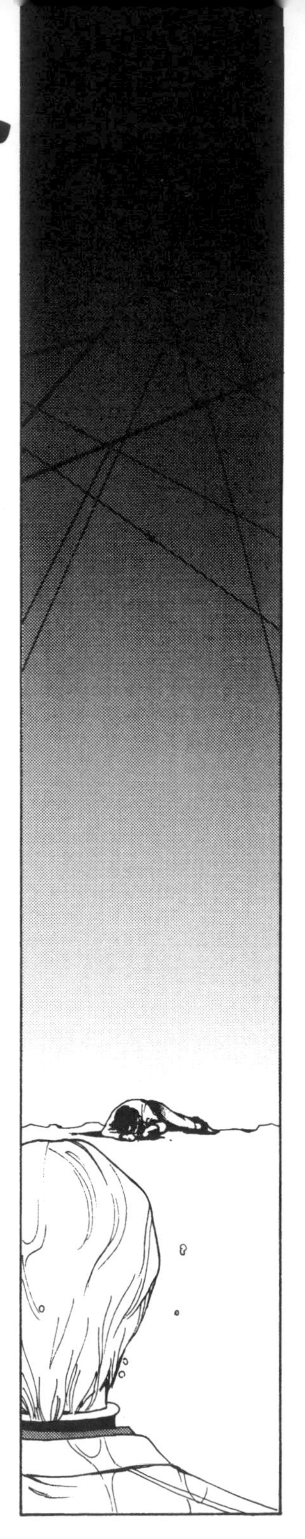

ZAAAAA
ZAAAAA
I'm not going back.

A Song From A Bird To Watch Over Me
Fearlessly, Unceasingly, Patiently
『見守る小鳥の歌』

A Place To Return To

I'm not going back.

Then where are you going to go?
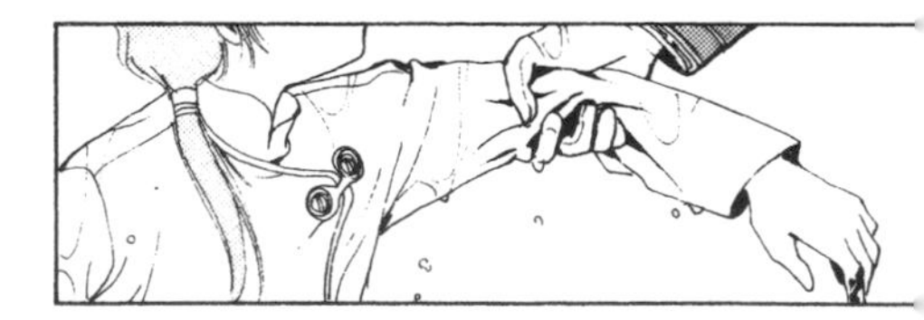

Klak
You don't want to catch a cold, do you?
No.
SLAM

RAIN
『雨』
あめ
It's raining.
That's good. It'll be cold.

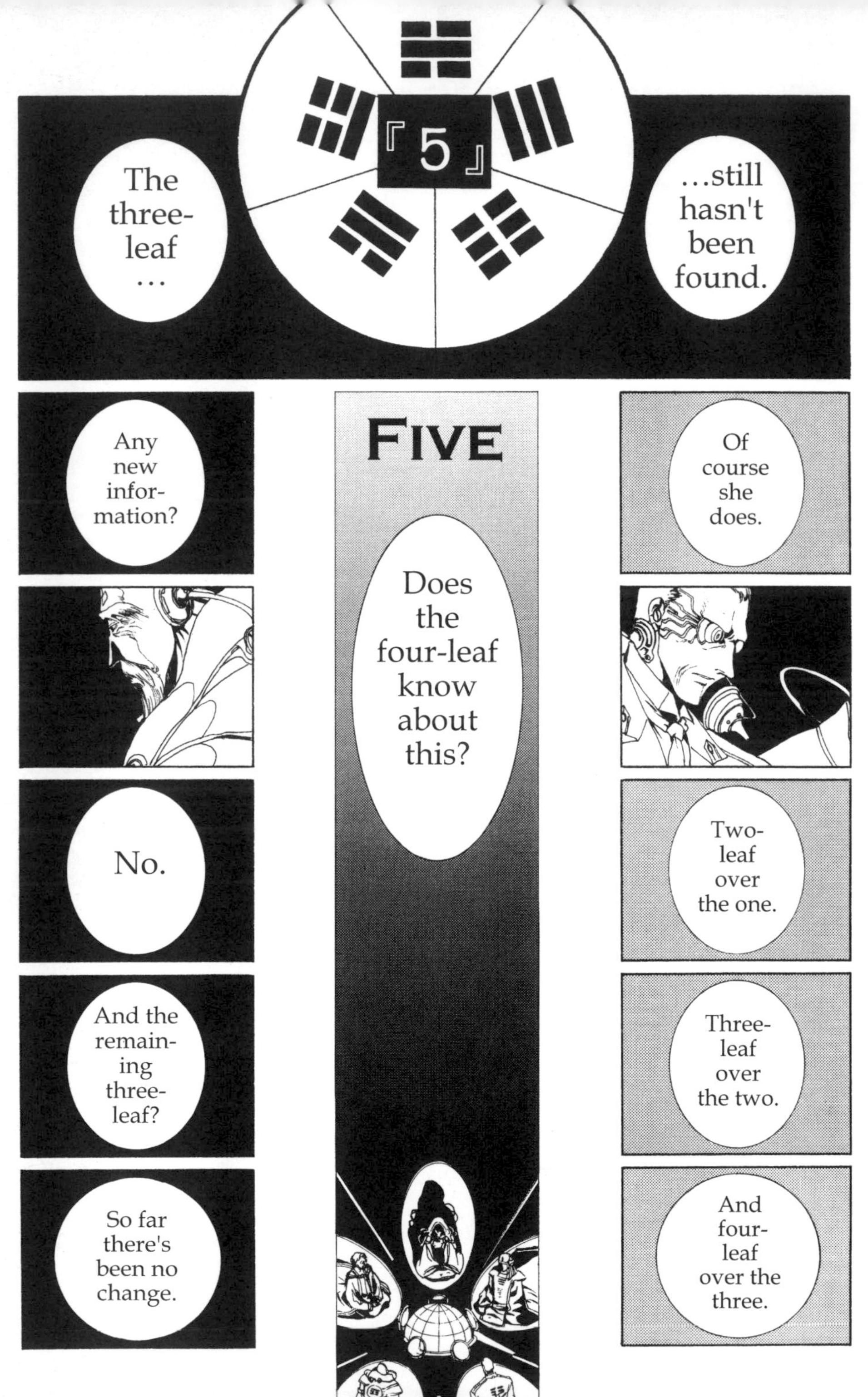
『5』
The three-leaf…
…still hasn't been found.
FIVE
Any new information?
No.
And the remaining three-leaf?
So far there's been no change.
Does the four-leaf know about this?
Of course she does.
Two-leaf over the one.
Three-leaf over the two.
And four-leaf over the three.

The more leafs, the stronger.

And the lower leafs don't have the ability to detect other Clovers or their powers.

But the higher leafs can track a lower leaf's position and determine its strengths.

She has kept her pact with us.
Impossible.
She will always be alone.
What if the three-leaf and the four-leaf should meet?
Doesn't that present a danger?
As far as the three-leaf is concerned, we can manage if the five of us combine our powers.

Besides, he cannot survive long outside the cage.
Clover
project.
3
Clover

『4』
FOUR
For you
I will be reborn
The bliss of our meeting
Is a gentle light
Our eventual parting a pouring rain
An indigo that blooms
In the delicate shade
In your arms
I will be reborn

clover leaf project.
3
Clover
You might be reborn.

THREE

『3』

What's this?

Did you want to stay wet?
No.
Is this yours?
No.
Do you like standing?
May I sit?
Do whatever you like.
You're military, right?
Yes.

What are you going to do with me?
What do you want me to do?
I never want to go back.
Why?

Because
A is
still
there.

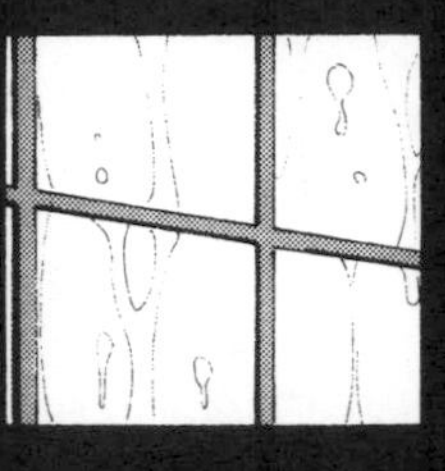

I'd like to speak to the Wizards.

TRUST

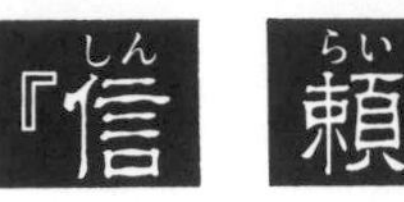

For
you

I will be
reborn

The bliss of our
meeting
Is a gentle light
Our eventual parting
a pouring rain

An indigo
that blooms
In the
delicate shade

In your arms
I will be reborn

You take
my hand
And I
hold yours
Our two paths cross as one
Deeply,
firmly
For myself
I will be reborn

In your arms
I will be reborn

No transmissions...
Blip
Blip
So, I assume that everything's alright.
Gingetsu.

DUTY
『任務』
I have the High Parlia-mentary Council Leader...
...Wizard Shu online.
Com-mander, please join us.

It's been many years, C.
So, you'd like to speak to me?
Time stands still in the cage.
Yes.
You know that B is dead.
Yes.
And I know how.
If I remain there, A will kill again.
Maybe you.
Is that what A said?

He and I are the only three-leaf Clovers.
He didn't say that.
But I know.
A said he would be able to leave if I was there to help him.

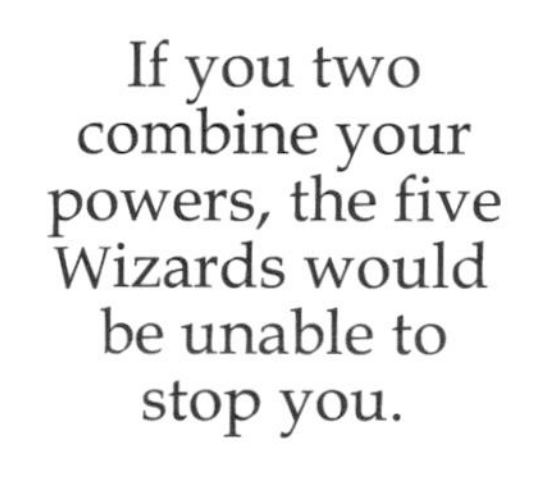
If you two combine your powers, the five Wizards would be unable to stop you.

I don't want that to happen.

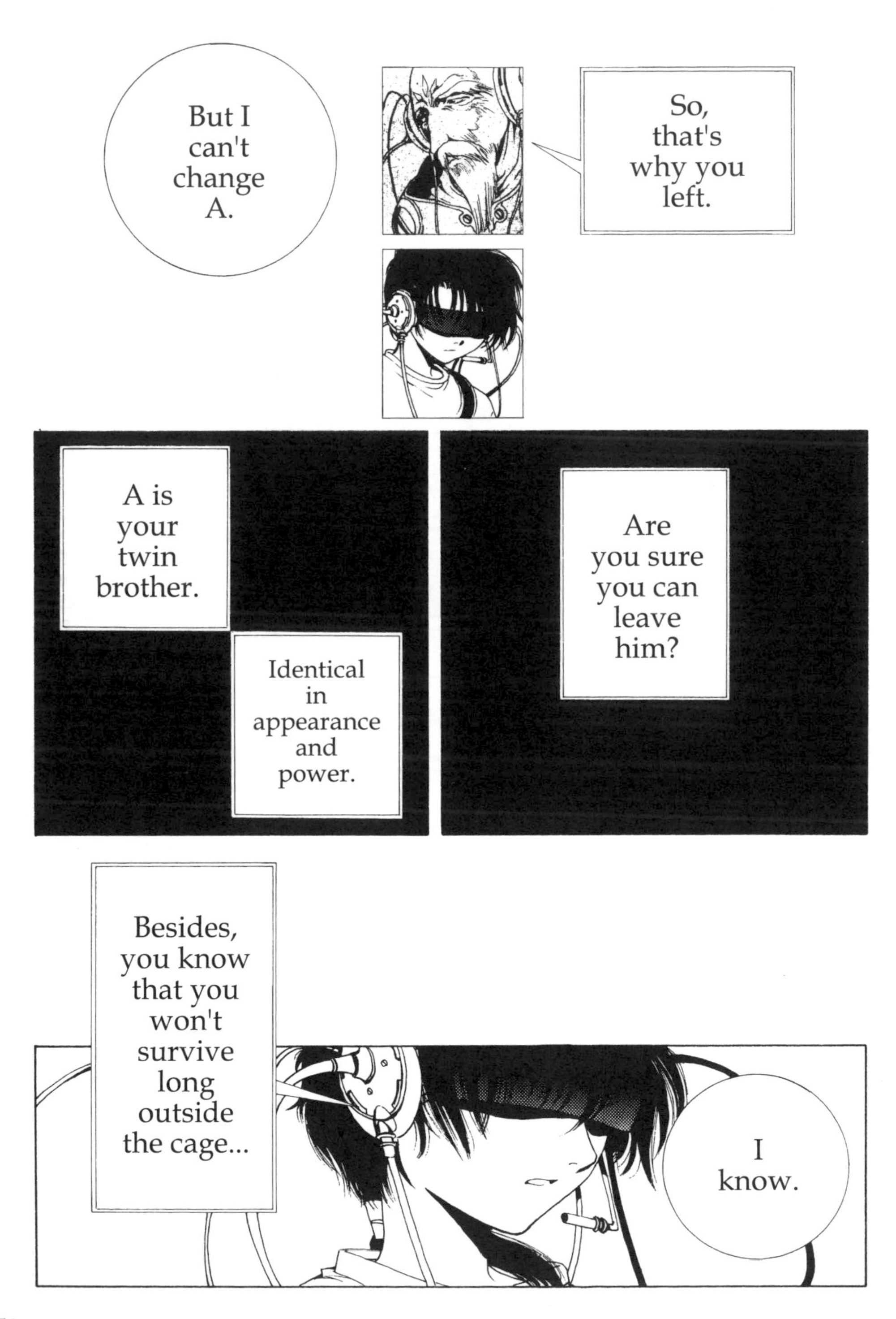
So, that's why you left.
But I can't change A.
A is your twin brother.
Identical in appearance and power.
Are you sure you can leave him?
Besides, you know that you won't survive long outside the cage...
I know.

A's emotions are unstable.

It probably is dangerous to keep you two together.

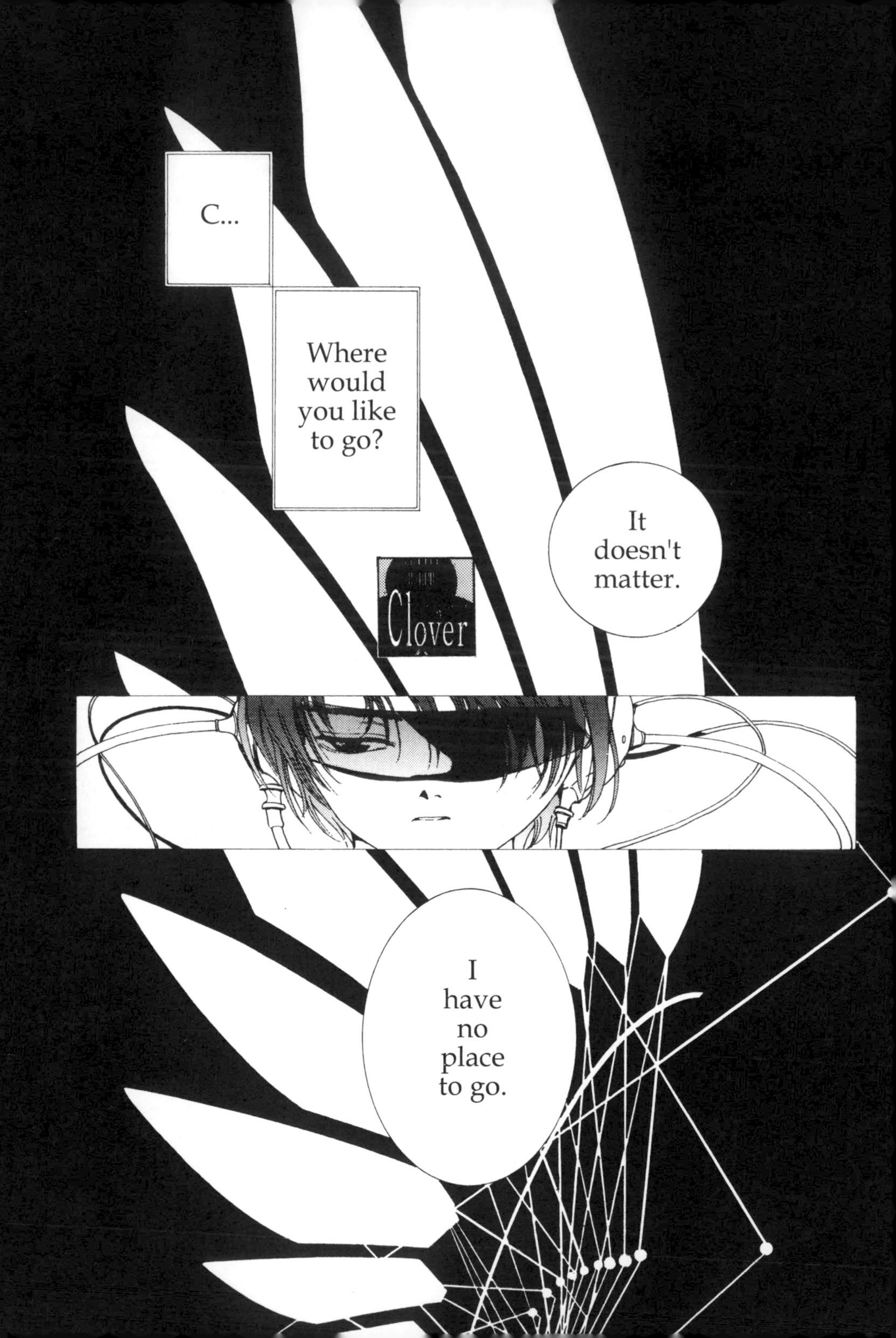
C...
Where would you like to go?
It doesn't matter.
Clover
I have no place to go.

Alright then. We'll look into the other three-leaf Clover.
Yes.
Is this an inconvenience?
Please look after the boy.
Commander Gingetsu.

Your orders are to protect the three-leaf Clover in your care.
Then it's a command.
Secret Service Unit Commander Gingetsu.
Yes, sir.

A Sign
『印』
しるし
What's the matter, C?
I guess something happened.
I know what you're feeling.
We were born together.

And we will always be together.

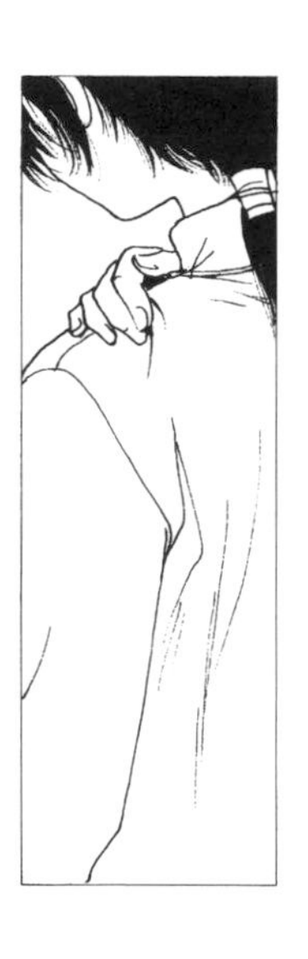

Always...
Forever...

For you
I will be reborn

『願（ねが）い』

A WISH

Don't look away

Never let go

The strength of will

The frailty of a wish

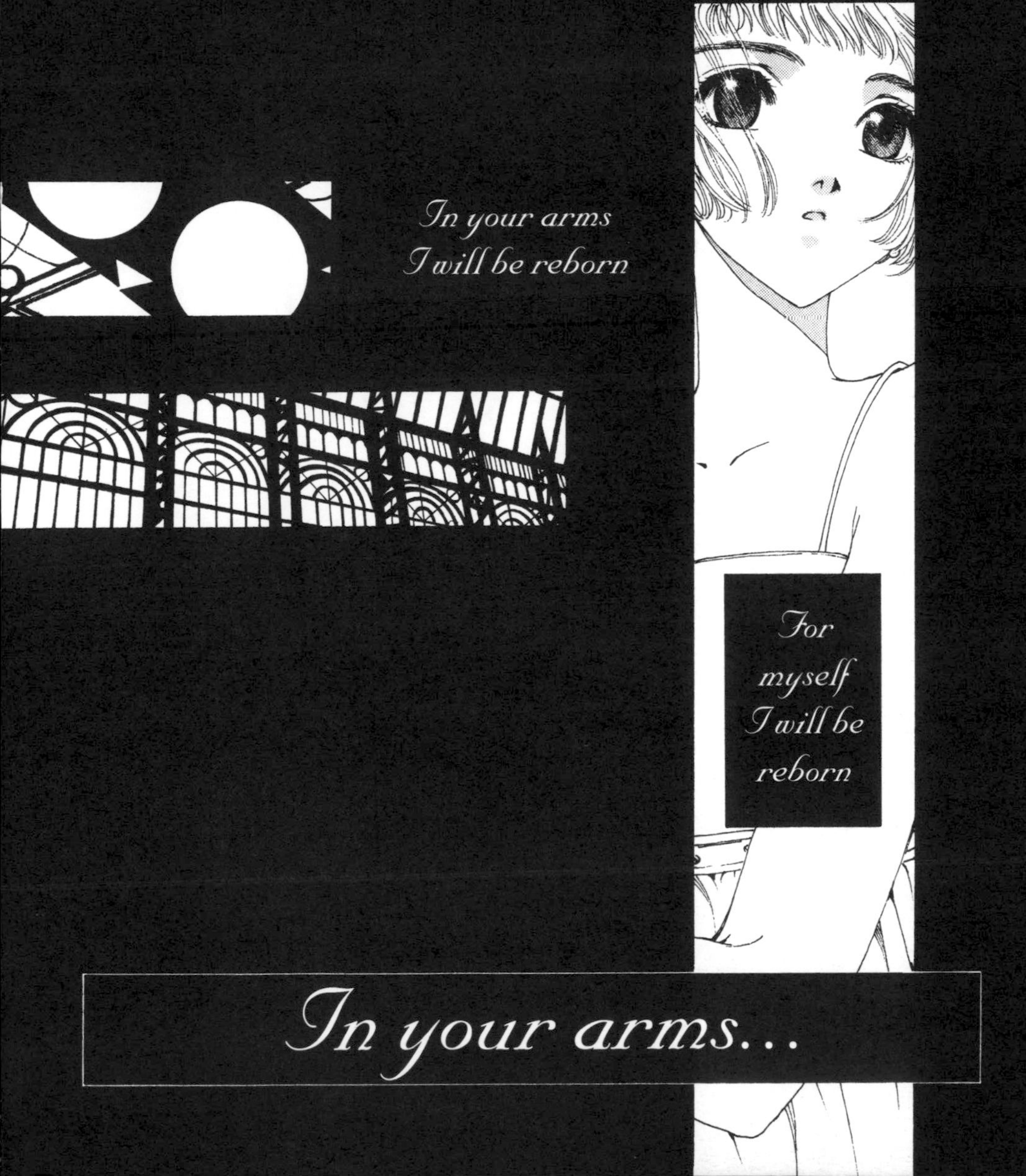
In your arms
I will be reborn
For
myself
I will be
reborn
In your arms...

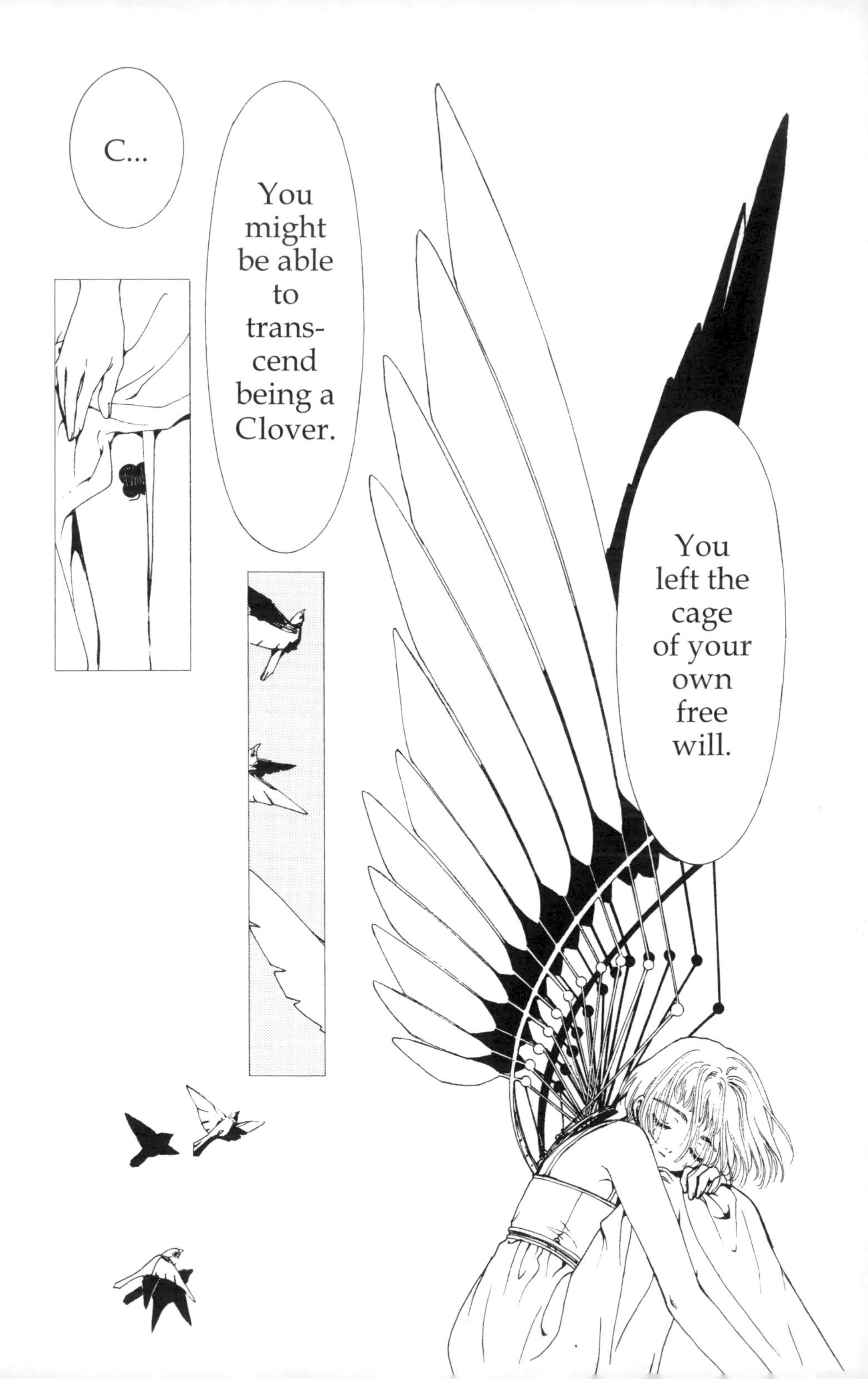
C...
You might be able to trans- cend being a Clover.
You left the cage of your own free will.

A Clover's Bliss

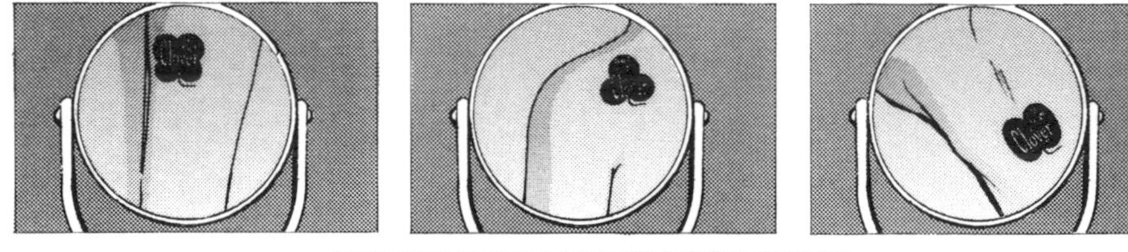

The Clover Leaf Project brandings?

They say you'll discover happiness if you find a clover.
But how will a Clover find happiness?
That is something the Clover will have to find out.

Soft Hair And Sweet Nothings

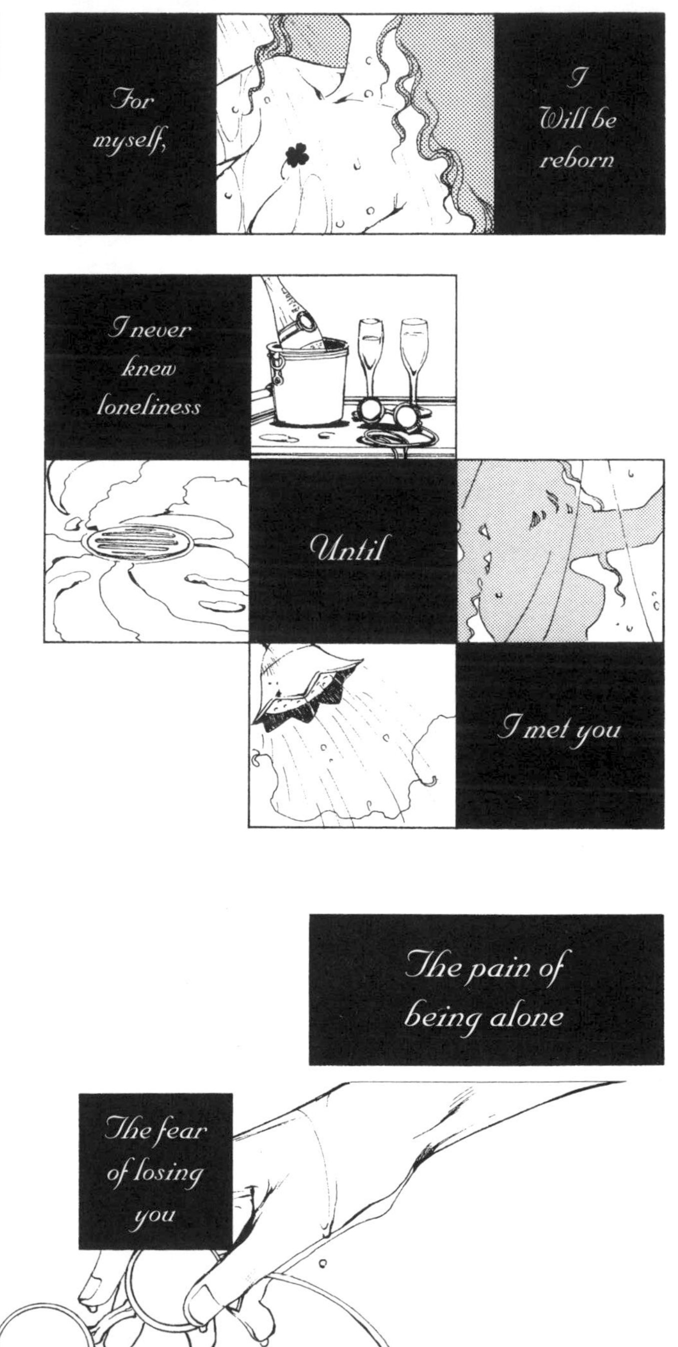

Thus, in your arms I will be reborn
For myself I will be reborn
beep-beep
In a bad mood?
Are you being called in?
Oh, no. It's nothing.

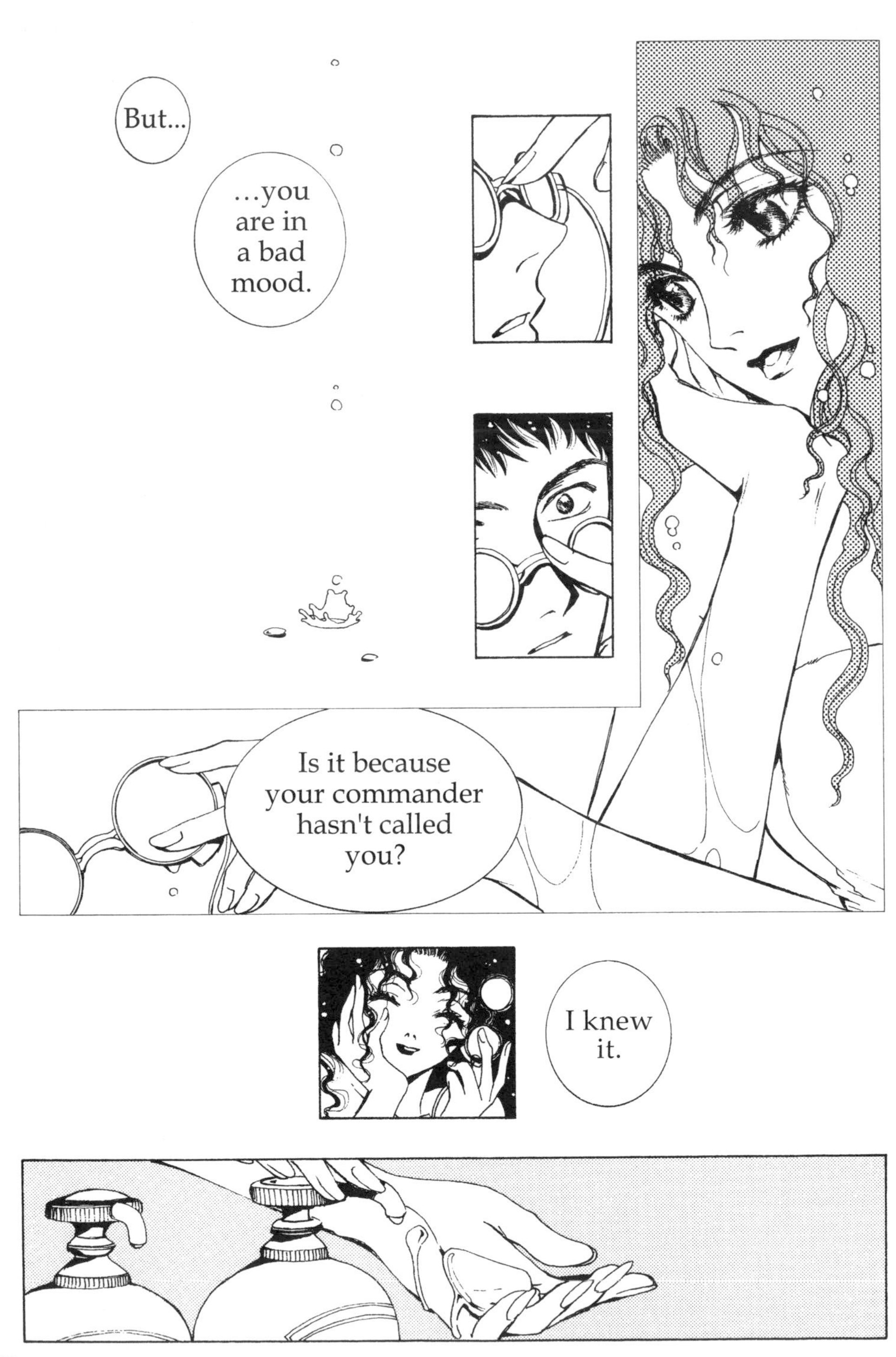
But...
...you are in a bad mood.
Is it because your commander hasn't called you?
I knew it.

Why do you want to wash my hair?
They say dogs don't like to appear vulnerable in front of enemies.
So, the fact that you're letting me wash you is proof that you love me.
So, you're saying I'm a dog?
I love you...
... Kazuhiko.

I want to stay...
...with you.
We will...
... always be together.

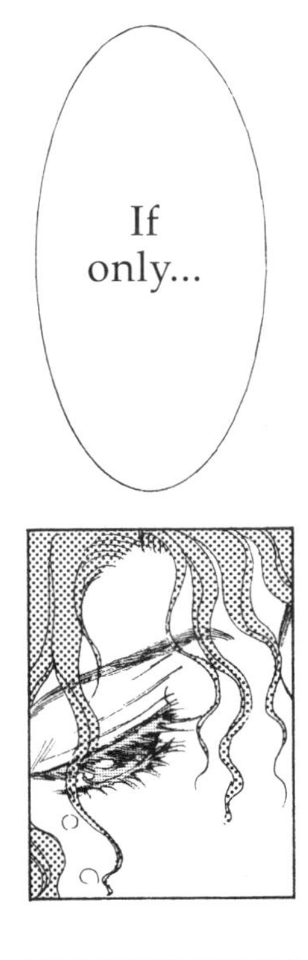
If only...

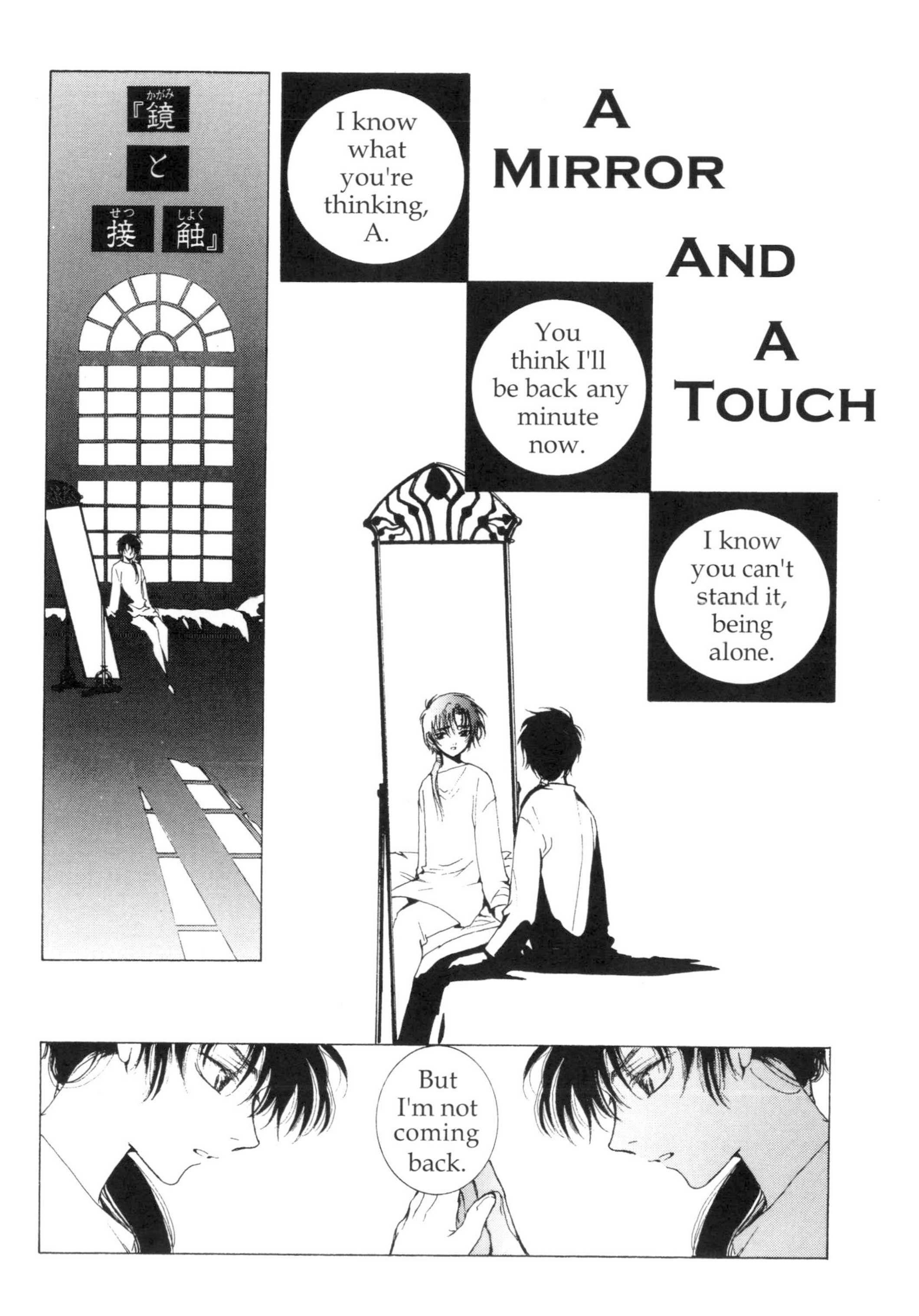
『鏡と接触』
A Mirror And A Touch
I know what you're thinking, A.
You think I'll be back any minute now.
I know you can't stand it, being alone.
But I'm not coming back.

A, even when we're together, it's like...
...I'm alone.
CRAASH

I'm sorry.
I broke your mirror.

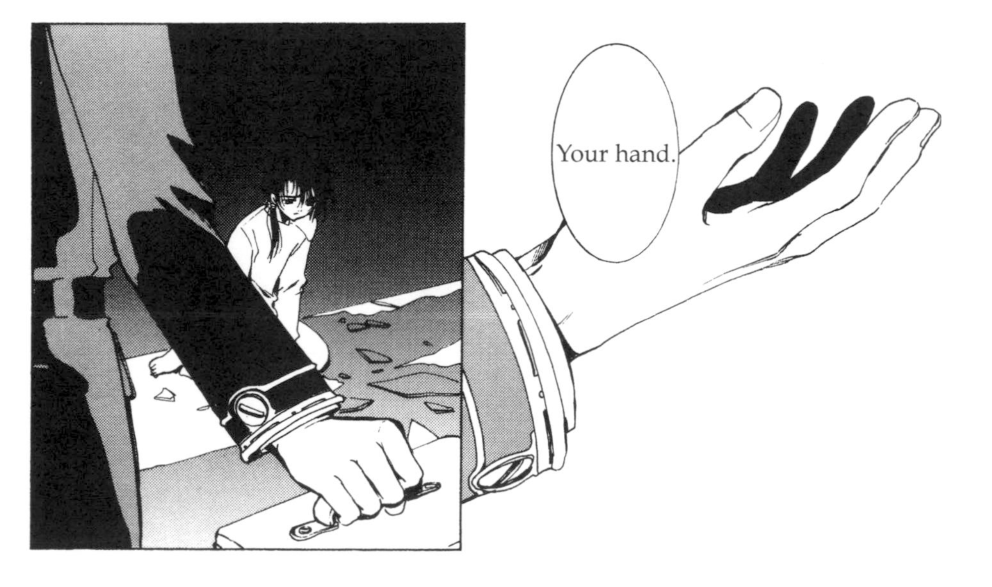
Your hand.

You're good at this.
Is it because of your work?
Thank you.
It's been awhile since I spoke to anyone other than A or B.
Do I talk too much?
Don't worry about it.

IRRITATION

『苛立ち』

I WANT TO SEE
『分からないから
I'm the only one who understands you.
How can you be happy without me?
Why so happy...
...C?

WHAT I DON'T UNDERSTAND

A Song For Everyone

『みんなにうたう歌(うた)』

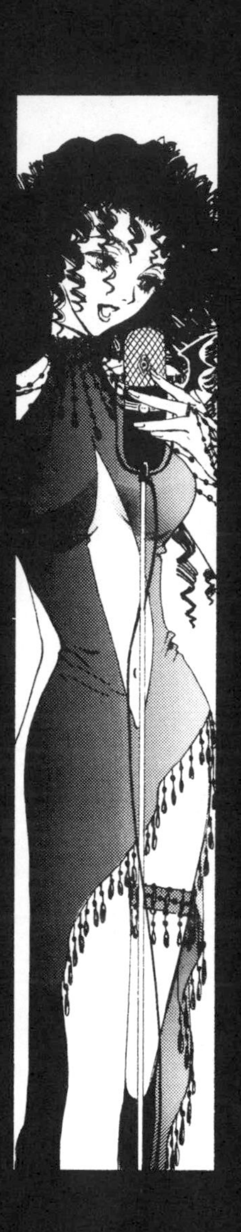

As I break off pieces of my old shell

Newly formed tears roll down my cheek

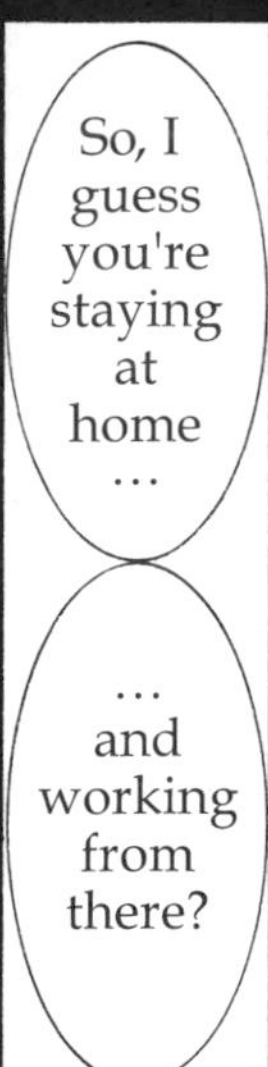

One of Shu's jobs?
That's right.
As you embrace me
My ethereal wings flutter open

Then I'll use my leave time and spend it with Ora.
Well, don't do anything I wouldn't do.
Unless, of course, it's really important.
Right.
See you.
Only for you
will I be reborn

『ふたりできく歌』
A Song For Two
It's a beautiful song.
I didn't mean to eavesdrop.
I can pick up the tiniest sounds.
Is she famous?
Not yet.
Oh.
Still...

...she sings beautifully.
In your arms
I will be reborn
Click
VOOM

Thank you.
I will be reborn

A Song For One
『ひとりでうたう歌』
As I break off pieces of my old shell
Newly formed tears roll down my cheek
In your arms
As you embrace me
My ethereal wings flutter open
It must be nice...
...to be outside the cage.

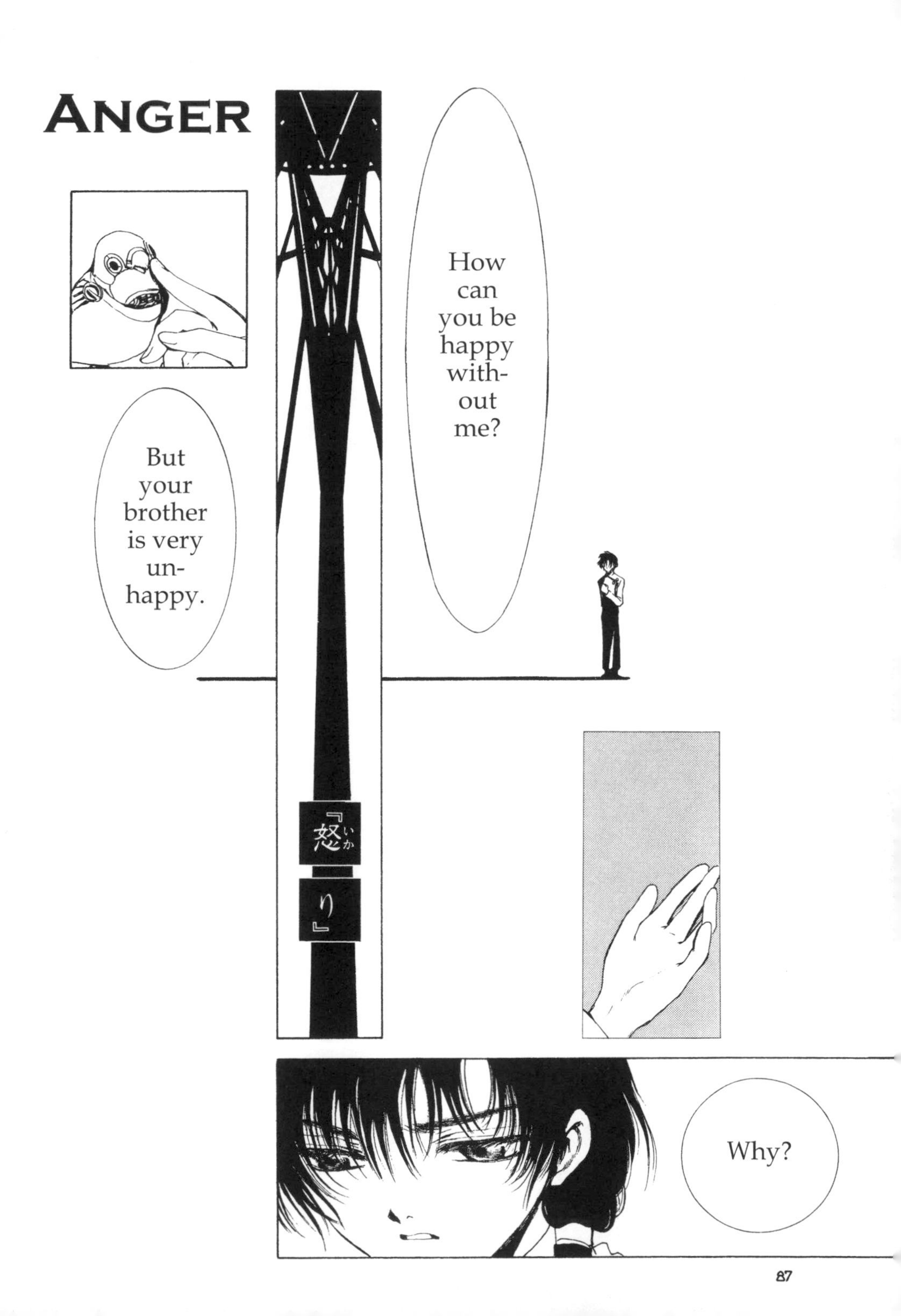
ANGER
How can you be happy without me?
But your brother is very unhappy.
『怒り』
Why?

『窓の外』
OUTSIDE THE WINDOW
In your arms
I will be reborn
For myself
I will be reborn

With a touch
of your hand
A whisper
of your voice
Let me forget
everything

Break off
the chains
that bind
My heart
and feet

How is C doing?
Well, so far.
C was always an obedient and well-behaved child.
But not so A.
A's emotions are fluctuating wildly.
He's not aware of the four-leaf's existence, so in his mind, he and C are the most powerful Clovers.
It might prompt him to take action.

Above all...
...he knows that he can't survive long outside the cage.
In your arms I will be reborn
For you I will be reborn

Do you want to go out-side?
No.
In your arms I will be reborn
For you I will be reborn

The lights are pretty, but they're not for me.

Not
ever...

『気を付けて』
Be careful!
BE CAREFUL
Your brother...

FAREWELL
『別れ』
...he's coming.

A hologram?

No, I'm the real thing.

Wait.

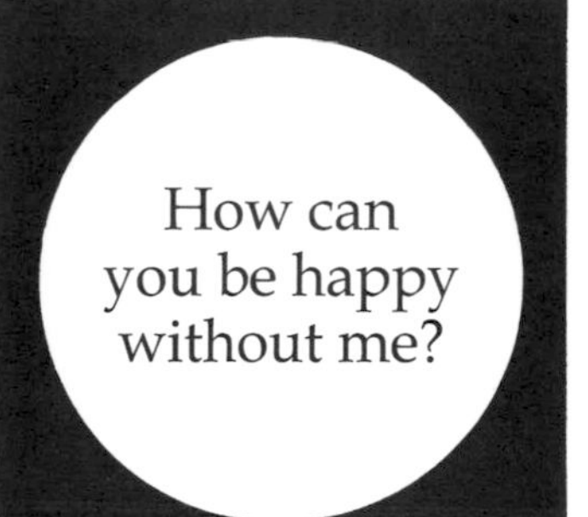
How can
you be happy
without me?

I'm not.

Then why are you here?

Is it because of him?

CRACKT
That's not it!
So, now you don't need me anymore?
A!

Get out of the way, C.
It's your fault. You wouldn't pay attention to me.
You loved B instead.
Just like I killed B.
I'm going to kill him.

I'll kill *myself* before I let you kill again.
No!

If we live apart, then we won't have to live in that cage.
Listen, A. As long as we're together…
…we're trapped.
I know what you're thinking, C.

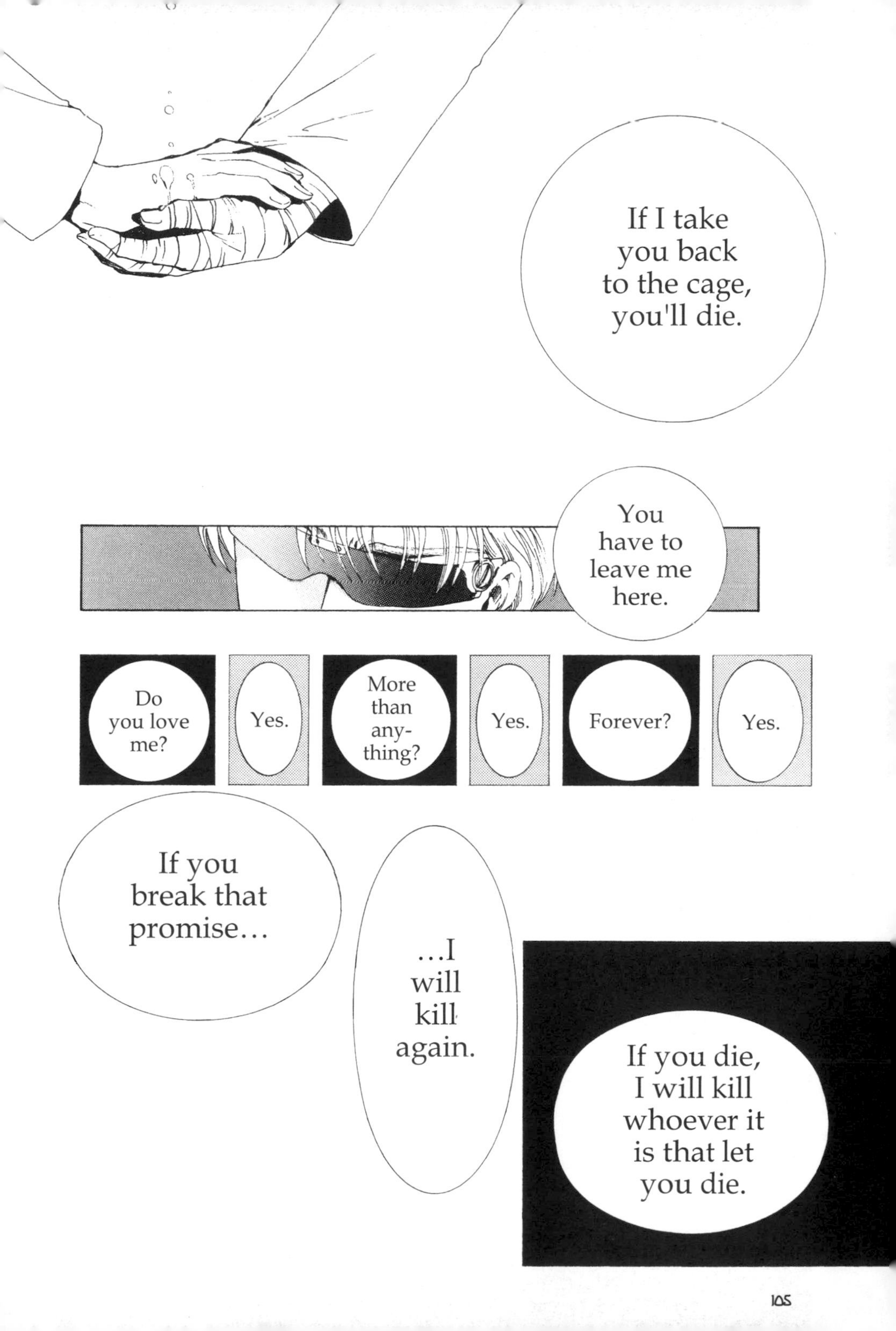
If I take you back to the cage, you'll die.
You have to leave me here.
Do you love me?
Yes.
More than any-thing?
Yes.
Forever?
Yes.
If you break that promise...
...I will kill again.
If you die, I will kill whoever it is that let you die.

I can feel your emotions, C. No matter where you are.

We're the only three-leafs on this earth.

I always will.

We'll always be linked together.

I'll see you ...

... Brother.

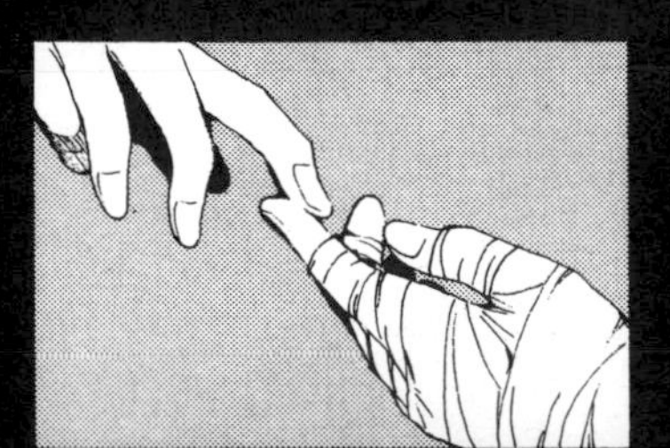

Good-
bye.

TEARS
『涙』
なみだ
I'm sorry.
I'll stop crying in a minute.
No.
You don't need my permission to cry.

Then do as you wish.
Thank you.

TWO-LEAF
『二葉』
ふた
ば
I heard A visited you.
Yes.
And C?
He said he would remain sepa-rated.
A said the same thing.
As long as they stay apart, we can keep them under control.
But we'll have to monitor their every move.
A is not stable, and is therefore unpredictable. It would be easier to monitor C.
Where?
It would have to be a location without access to the outside.

But you're a two-leaf.

There's no way I can allow you to coexist with a three-leaf.

Two plus three equals five.

Combined, you two could overpower the Council.

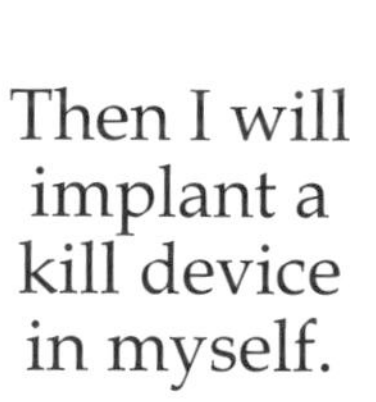

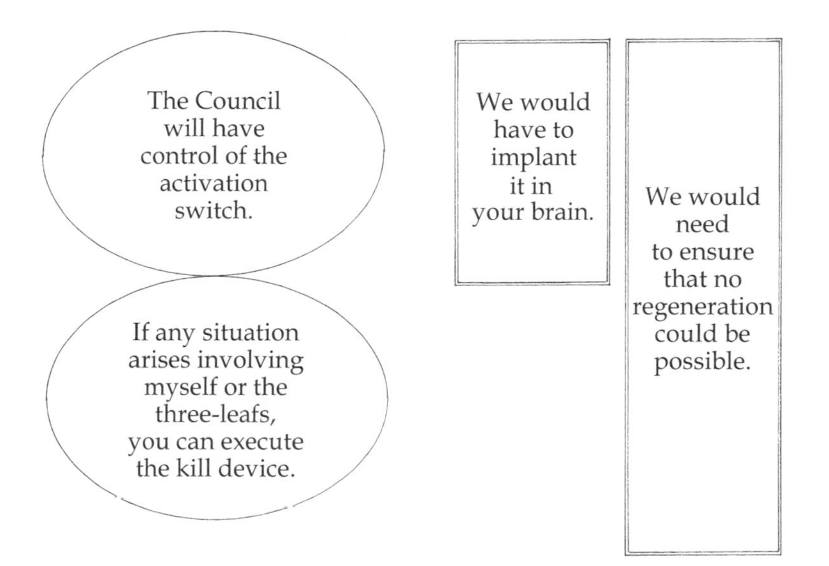
We would have to implant it in your brain.
We would need to ensure that no regeneration could be possible.
The Council will have control of the activation switch.
If any situation arises involving myself or the three-leafs, you can execute the kill device.

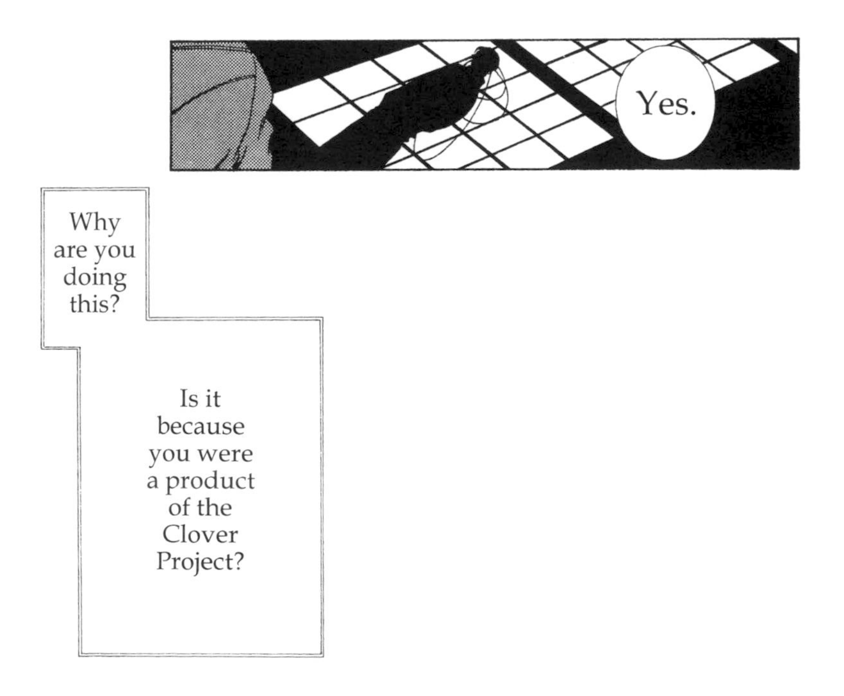
Yes.
Why are you doing this?
Is it because you were a product of the Clover Project?

Especially since adjutant Kazuhiko Ryu's arrival under your command.

The Gingetsu I know would never do this.

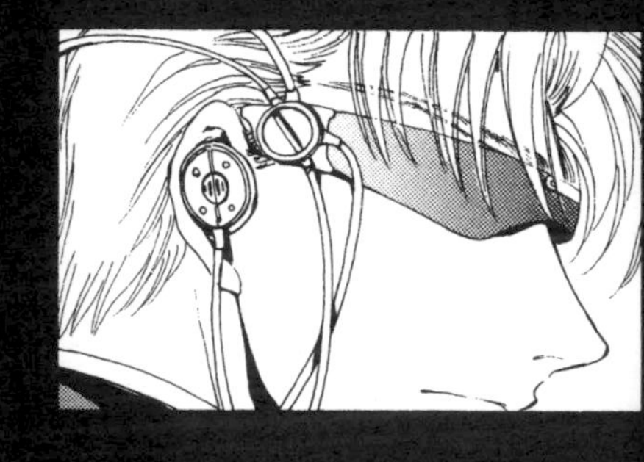

I just decided that this would be the best way to handle the situation.

You've changed, my boy.

As you know, the three-leafs cannot survive long outside the cage.

They will begin to undergo accelerated aging. At best, they'll have five years.

I understand.

Thank you for everything.

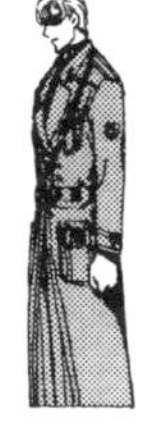

What?
As long as you stay inside...
...the Council will allow it.
But ...!
You're a two-leaf, aren't you?!
Clover
2
clover leaf project
It's going to put you in trouble!
Are you planning to make trouble?
No, but...!
Do you have anywhere else to go?

I want to stay here!

Then stay.

Thank you...

C → R
『C ツェー
R ラン』
So, finally I hear from you.
I ended up covering for you the whole time.
If you want to make up for it, you better taste-test my cooking.
Who's this?
You into little kids now?
I was planning to cook for Ora, but I'm not ready yet. So you're my test subject.
This is Ran.
I'm Kazuhiko Fay Ryu. You can call me Kazuhiko.
What's your name?

Nice name.
Well, nice meeting you, Ran.
I'm gonna start cooking.
If it's dark, you can always turn the lights on.
In your arms, I will be reborn

For you I will be reborn
An ember just lit
Let it not be put out

My thoughts
just created
May they not
be forgotten

Watch over this cradle
I begin again from nothing
For myself I will be reborn

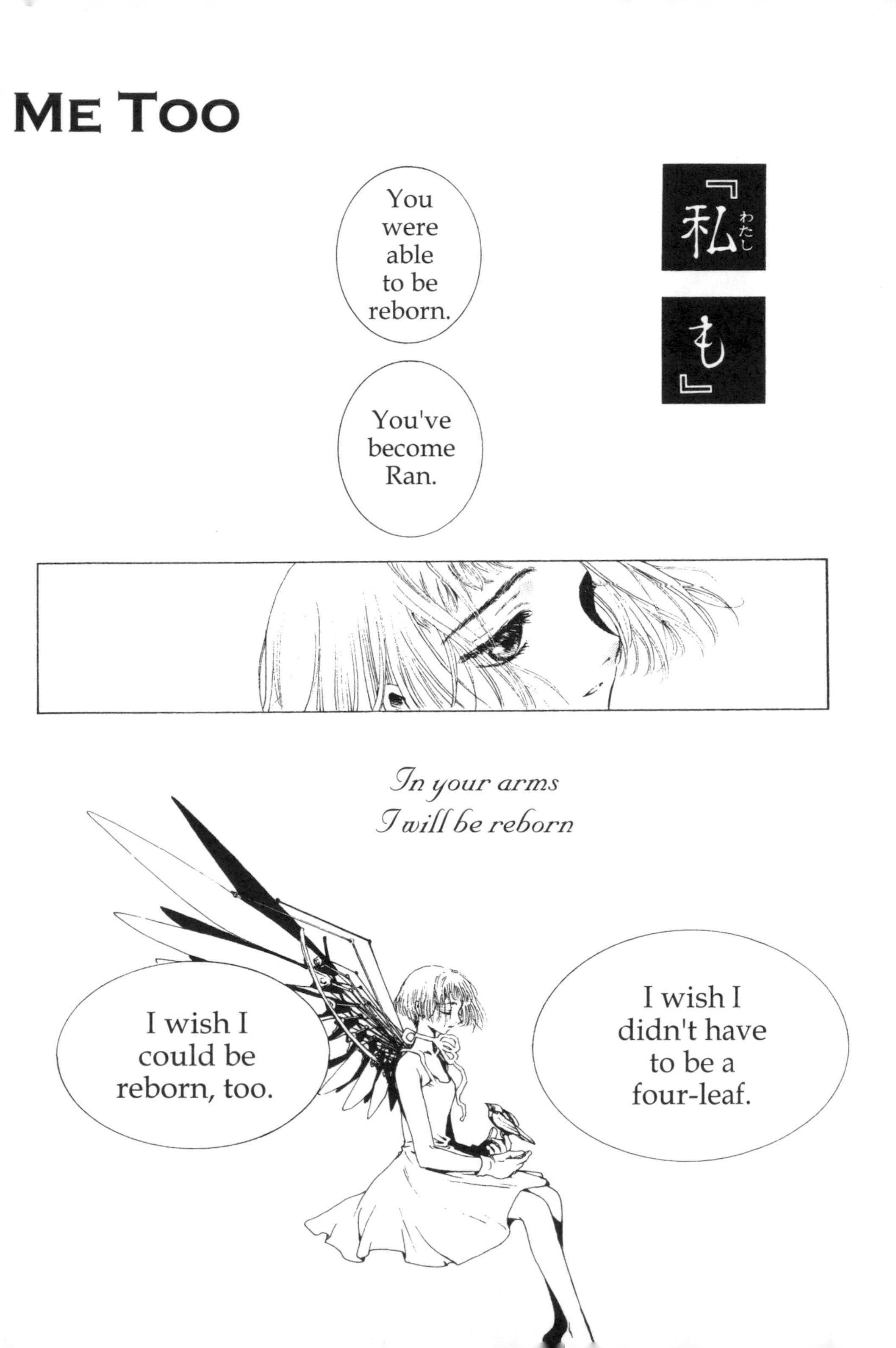
ME TOO
『私(わたし)も』
You were able to be reborn.
You've become Ran.
In your arms
I will be reborn
I wish I didn't have to be a four-leaf.
I wish I could be reborn, too.

If you find a four-leaf clover
You will discover
happiness

But
It can never be found

Happiness lies inside
A secret cage

No one can possess
The four-leaf clover

PLANNING+PRESENT+BOOK DESIGN

STORY

NANASE OHKAWA (CLAMP)

COMIC

もこな あぱぱ

MOKONA APAPA (CLAMP)

ASSISTANTS

五十嵐 さつき

SATSUKI IGARASHI (CLAMP)

猫井 みっく

MICK NEKOI (CLAMP)

LOGOTYPE•DIGITAL EFFECT

須予 博方

HIROMASA SUKO (PAP studio tria)

菊地 等

HITOSHI KIKUCHI (PAP studio tia)

ENGLISH TRANSLATION

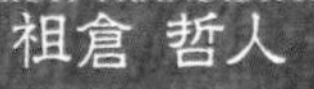

TETSUTO SOKURA

EDITOR

山之内 秀樹

HIDEKI YAMANOUCHI (KODANSHA)

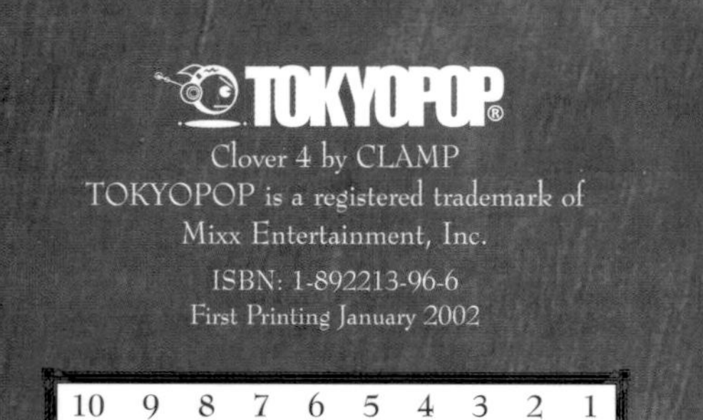

TOKYOPOP®
Clover 4 by CLAMP
TOKYOPOP is a registered trademark of
Mixx Entertainment, Inc.
ISBN: 1-892213-96-6
First Printing January 2002

10 9 8 7 6 5 4 3 2 1

Translator - Ray Yoshimoto. Retouch Artist - Bernard San Juan.
Graphic Assistants - Anna Kernbaum and Thea Willis. Graphic Designer - Akemi Imafuku.
Editors - Robert Coyner and Stephanie Donnelly. Senior Editor - Jake Forbes.
Production Manager - Fred Lui. Art Director - Matt Alford.
VP of Production - Ron Klamert. Publisher - Stu Levy.

Email: editor@press.TOKYOPOP.com
Come visit us at www.TOKYOPOP.com

TOKYOPOP®
Los Angeles - Tokyo